Original title:
Life's Big Questions, Answered by Your Dog

Copyright © 2025 Creative Arts Management OÜ
All rights reserved.

Author: Ophelia Ravenscroft
ISBN HARDBACK: 978-1-80566-094-1
ISBN PAPERBACK: 978-1-80566-389-8

The Art of the Wag

When you ask me what is true,
Just look at my tail, it wags for you.
The secret of joy is quite plain,
It's in chasing squirrels, not in the strain.

In the darkest moments, don't despair,
A belly rub can show you care.
Am I wise? That's hard to say,
But treats and naps always save the day.

A Dog's Perspective

Life is simple, or so it seems,
Chase your dreams and follow beams.
Fetch the stick and drop the ball,
Happiness is the best of all.

Sniff the ground, what secrets lie?
Is it pizza crust from nearby?
Humans ponder, fret, and moan,
But I'm just happy chewing a bone.

Scenting the Answers

What's the meaning of it all?
I just know there's a great big ball.
A stick, a park, a sunny day,
Now that feels like a doggone way.

When you frown, just take a breath,
With my big eyes, I'll save you from death.
We'll play tug and forget the woes,
As long as I get those yummy bones.

Barking at the Stars

Why do you look up at the night?
There's nothing there but a silly light.
While you think deep thoughts, I'm here,
Barking at a shadow, a squirrel near.

In the cosmic dance, I find my place,
Chasing dreams at a playful pace.
So forget the worries, let's have a spree,
The stars can wait while you pet me.

Howling at the Heart of Existence

When the moon is high and bright,
  I chase my tail, what a sight!
   Wagging fur is my delight,
  Wondering if socks are right.

  Philosophy's a bone to chew,
   Is it really fun for you?
  Tiles or grass, what's the view?
Let's keep it simple, that's the cue.

Joy in the Simple Acts of Being

Squirrels dart and birds take flight,
Chasing joy feels so right.
Every walk's a pure delight,
Rolling in leaves, blissful white.

With a stick, I find my peace,
In the sun, all worries cease.
Silly hats, my heart's increase,
Loving life is my expertise.

Canine Clarity on Humanity's Path

Fetch the ball or sit and stay,
Humans worry, while I play.
Licking faces, come what may,
  Do we really need a say?

Paws on earth and nose to sky,
Chasing truth as time flies by.
If you ask me, no need to lie,
  Just be happy, woof and sigh.

Pawprints on Our Journey

Every step, a planned embrace,
Through the park, a joyful race.
Each new friend gives me a chase,
Sniffing out the right place.

When the sun sets, I will lay,
Dreaming of bones that greet the day.
Life's a treat, come what may,
Together, let's just play away.

The Essence of Trust in a Dog's Gaze

When you stare deep into my eyes,
You'll find a truth that's oh so wise.
I may not speak, but I understand,
Your laughter fills the air, so grand.

With a wag of my tail, I can say,
Your worries vanish, come what may.
In sunlit days or rainy gloom,
My joyful barks chase away the gloom.

You ponder questions, loop and twirl,
Yet in my world, it's simply pearl.
Just toss the ball, let's run and play,
Your cares dissolve, they drift away.

So trust your heart, let worries cease,
For in my gaze, you'll find your peace.
Together we'll roam, both wild and free,
In a bond that's pure, just you and me.

A Companionship of Questions and Joys

What's the meaning of this strange ride?
With treats in the bag and you by my side.
I sniff the ground, you ponder the stars,
Our adventures sprinkled with laughs and jars.

Is the mailman friend or foe?
I bark loud, and you say, 'Let's go!'
Chasing squirrels, both fast and spry,
Who needs answers? Just watch us fly!

Why do you frown when I roll in dirt?
Isn't it fun? Wouldn't it hurt?
When worries chase you like a pack,
I'll lay my head upon your back.

So toss the questions, let's dig and play,
In my world there's always a way.
With you, my friend, the road's a joy,
Together forever, girl and boy!

Unraveled by a Dog's Gaze

In the morning light, you stare,
With your bright eyes, without a care.
Why bark at shadows, oh wise one?
Because they're there, and barking's fun!

In the park, you chase the breeze,
Fetch a stick with such great ease.
What's the meaning of this game?
It's simple, buddy—just the same!

Sniffs of Certainty Amidst Chaos

A whiff of grass, a sniff of dirt,
You pause to ponder—what's my shirt?
Why roll in mud, with glee, my friend?
To feel alive, on that you can depend!

You dash through puddles, oh so spry,
Is this joy? You give a sigh.
What's the secret of your grin?
It's all about the fun within!

A Canvas of Fur and Thought

With fur as soft as clouds up high,
You wear your thoughts, oh my, oh my!
Why chase your tail, round and round?
It's a masterpiece of joy you've found!

You sit and watch the world go by,
Is there a reason? Yes, oh my!
You tilt your head, curious and wise,
Because life's a mystery wrapped in surprise!

Pondering Life With a Playful Heart

With wagging tail, you greet the dawn,
What was that sound? Just a lawn!
Why bark at squirrels in the tree?
They're plotting schemes—that's clear to me!

You leap and bound, in pure delight,
Is there a question? Just hold tight!
What's your wisdom in this play?
Joy's the answer, come what may!

The Love That Knows No Boundaries

With wagging tails and playful barks,
My heart expands, it gleams and sparks.
Unconditional love without a fight,
You smile at me, and the world's so bright.

Through muddy paws and slobbery kisses,
You teach me joy, like energy in the blisses.
A friend so loyal, always near,
In your presence, I lose all fear.

Enigmas Wrapped in Fur

What do you think when squirrels appear?
Do you wonder if they're out of here?
Your puzzled look cracks me up so deep,
In the chaos of chase, there's no time for sleep.

Around your bowl, secrets abound,
Your eyes, like mirrors, with wisdom profound.
From your playful prance to your thoughtful stare,
In your furry enigma, love lays bare.

The Lightness of Being Canine

When life's weight seems like a chore,
You bound outside, ask for more.
With a leap and a bark, you take to the sky,
Showing me how to live high and dry.

A scratch behind the ears brings peace,
In your world, all worries cease.
Napping in sunbeams, you show me the way,
To take it easy, savor the day.

Searching for Answers in the Barking Crowd

In a sea of woofs, the language is loud,
Each bark a question, a playful crowd.
What's out there? Is it mine?
I see you sniff, it must be divine!

From ball to stick, the quest unfolds,
Can have and have-not be told in gold?
Through all the noise and yappy cheer,
Your simple joy lights the path clear.

Fur-etched Answers

What is the meaning? Go fetch the ball,
Joy in simple things, we can have a ball.
When food is near, the mystery fades,
You'll cherish the treats, as laughter invades.

Paws to the ground, sniffing the air,
With a wagging tail, showing us flair.
Questions dissolve in a swirl of fun,
With every bark, a new smile is won.

Beneath the Wagging Tail

Why chase the squirrels? They won't be caught,
A game of chase, the best fun we've wrought.
Will I find truth in a scratch behind ears?
Every wiggle says, 'Chase away fears!'

Beneath that wag, there's wisdom unwrapped,
With playful nudges, all worries are lapped.
Life is a game, as we leap and bound,
In the heart of a pup, true joy is found.

The Sound of Loyalty

What is true friendship? It's all in the eyes,
A tail that wags, never full of lies.
In puddles we splash, together we roam,
In a world of wonder, we both call home.

Barking at shadows, they vanish in glee,
Chasing our dreams, just you and me.
With every woof, an answer appears,
A chorus of loyalty, laughter, and cheers.

Whispers from the Leash

Is the grass greener? Just take a sniff,
On this grand adventure, let's take a lift.
In every park, there's magic we find,
With every wag, open hearts unwind.

What makes you happy? A roll in the sun,
With belly upturned, we both just have fun.
In the laughter shared, the worries will cease,
From the bark of a dog, we find our peace.

The Art of Living According to Dogs

Chase your tail, round and round,
Worry not when lost, just found.
Naps are king, your throne awaits,
Bark at strangers, celebrate!

Socks are treasures, chew with glee,
Sing and dance, live wild and free.
Find joy in mud, roll in the grass,
All your worries? Let them pass.

Reflections in a Puddle of Drool

Look in that puddle, what do you see?
A face so wise, as wise can be.
The world is big, with scents so grand,
Each new adventure, just take my hand.

Why ponder life? Just fetch that ball!
The meaning of it? Just have a ball!
Drool on my chin, it's a badge of pride,
Wagging my tail, you're by my side.

Through the Eyes of a Canine Sage

In the quiet corners, I ponder fate,
As mailman approaches, don't hesitate!
With a tilt of my head, I ask the stars,
Why do humans drive in those metal cars?

When friends are near, the worries cease,
Cuddles and treats, a moment of peace.
Fetch is life, and life is fetch,
Drop the thoughts, come join the sketch.

Treats and Transcendence

Treats fall from heaven, wrapped in delight,
Just one more please, I'll be polite!
Chasing my tail? It's a workout too,
Elation in leaps, like you wouldn't do!

Every bark carries a wise refrain,
Get up, go out, and dance in the rain!
Happiness bubbles, like water in bowls,
In the end, it's love that consoles.

The Depth of a Dog's Gaze

In your eyes, I see the world,
A squirrel, a tree, my tail unfurled.
You ponder deep thoughts, oh so wide,
I just want treats, and a sunny slide.

Unspoken Bonds and Unanswered Thoughts

You ask the stars, what's out there?
I chase my tail without a care.
Your worries grow like weeds in June,
I dream of bones beneath the moon.

Paws and the Great Unknown

You stare at maps, paths to roam,
I sniff the grass, my favorite home.
With every bark, a quest unfolds,
While I just seek the hugs you hold.

Cuddles that Challenge Perspective

You dive in books, explore the pages,
I dive in laps, where love engages.
Philosophy, or just a glance?
To me, it's all about the chance!

Paws of Wisdom

Why chase the mailman, my dear friend?
A squirrel's laugh will never end.
Bark at the moon, let it hear your voice,
In a world of treats, we all rejoice.

Sniff the grass, oh what a thrill,
Nature provides the best kind of chill.
Fetch the stick, don't worry 'bout speed,
Sometimes simplicity meets every need.

Life's a game of tug-of-war,
With every win, you'll want more.
A belly rub can solve it all,
From a small snack, we never stall.

So take a leap, and grab a toy,
For every moment, we'll share the joy.
In every wag, there's wisdom to find,
Laughter and love, joyfully entwined.

The Unspoken Truths of Tails

What do you see when you glance at me?
A heart that's wild and ever free.
Each wagging tail tells a tale so grand,
From the hopes we chase to the treats at hand.

Why fret about days that pass so fast?
Roll in the grass, let your worries cast.
Chase your dreams like squirrels in flight,
With every bark, we'll make things right.

In the puddles, let's jump and splash,
Forget the time, let's make a dash.
A cozy nook is where we align,
All the world's puzzles, we always find.

So grab the leash, let's take a stroll,
Two curious souls, who make each other whole.
Unravel the mysteries of every park,
Together we roam, with laughter and bark.

Echoes in the Bark

What's in the bark that stirs the air?
A voice of joy, beyond compare.
Each echo carries a playful cheer,
Bringing laughter, chasing every fear.

When the sky is gray, chase away gloom,
Play fetch with shadows that dance in the room.
Roll in the leaves, let the season spin,
Every moment's a treasure that we win.

What do you want when you ask for a treat?
To know that life's simple, and oh, so sweet.
But don't forget the cuddles at play,
In love and wagging tails, we find our way.

So let the world be a stage today,
With every bark, let worries decay.
For in this bond, we've found our spark,
As we create music in every mark.

Canine Philosophies

Why sit and ponder on what's ahead?
Chase the sun instead, let worries shed.
A frisbee's flight speaks of freedom's song,
In every bark, you'll find where you belong.

What do you seek in each juicy bone?
The taste of joy, in every groan.
In naps and dreams, we find our peace,
Each wagging tail is a sweet release.

Let's wander far where the wildflowers grow,
With every sniff, let our hearts overflow.
What matters most is not where we roam,
It's the warmth of a hug that feels like home.

So come, let's bark ideas in the breeze,
For wisdom is found in wagging with ease.
In every paw print, a path we'll explore,
Together we shine, forever we soar.

Truths Known Only to Four-Legged Friends

When the mailman comes, don't you fret,
Just bark loud like you're a household threat.
Those squirrels outside? They're all in on it,
Keep barking, my friend, don't you ever quit.

Your food's the best, it's rich and divine,
While I eat green beans, thinking they're fine.
My shoes are tasty, I just want a bite,
But who cares, let's play, it'll be alright!

Chasing tails is fun, a game of pure glee,
I question why you all can't join me.
Silly humans, with your strange little ways,
Life's simple joys, in a dog's endless play.

Love is a ball, it's round and it bounces,
Sometimes it comes from odd doggie trounces.
Just roll on the floor, let worries depart,
In a wagging tail, you'll find the true heart.

The Comfort of Canine Companionship

When you're feeling down, I'll lay by your feet,
For a puppy hug, nothing can beat.
Snuggles and kisses, I'm your furry mate,
In this vast universe, we'll create our fate.

You say life's hard? Let's take a quick nap,
Dream of big bones and a comfy dog flap.
Your couch is my throne, your heart is my bone,
Together we'll laugh, never alone!

Let's chase around, those worries behind,
The world seems better, with a friend so kind.
Sniffing each flower, just stopping to play,
In our secret kingdom, we'll spend every day.

So when life gets tough, please look into my eyes,
I'll remind you of joy, and that's no surprise.
With barks and with wagging, we'll conquer it all,
Your pup by your side, we're having a ball!

Walks Through Wonder and Worry

Each walk is a quest, let's explore the ground,
With every new scent, adventure's around.
Big trees are for sniffing, mailboxes to greet,
Every step is a story, each path is a treat.

The world is a puzzle, a leash in your hand,
I'm the guide dog here; together we'll stand.
The sky is so big and the grass is so green,
Tell me your troubles, I'm yours, I'm your machine.

Oh look, there's a cat! Quick, give me a chase,
Life's a mad sprint, let's pick up the pace!
We'll play by the park and roll in the mud,
Forgetting our worries, just having some fun.

With each wag of my tail, I dispel all your fears,
In this grand adventure, you'll find joy through tears.
So step out with me, there's magic in trots,
Through wonder and worry, together we'll plot.

A Cuddle and a Cosmic Question

In the quiet of night, let's cuddle real tight,
While you ponder life's meaning — we'll hold the light.
Why do you humans love counting stars?
Meanwhile, I'm just happy chasing my paws.

Is there a doggie heaven where pizzas do roam?
Where all your socks are safe, and laughter's a home?
With biscuits aplenty, and naps in the sun,
Why worry when joy resembles a run?

Would you like to learn the secrets I know?
How chasing your tail really puts on a show!
The universe winks, as you scratch my tummy,
Oh, the deep thoughts we share — they're quite funny!

In this cuddle and warmth, we ponder away,
Furry and wise, we'll chase dark clouds to stray.
So curl up with me, and feel the grace pause,
Together we'll laugh, the world's full of paws!

Wisdom in Every Sit and Stay

When you sit, oh dog so wise,
You ponder treats of every size.
With a tilt of head and wagging tail,
You teach us love will always prevail.

In a world of fetch, you find your peace,
With every bark, you claim your lease.
The sofa's throne, your kingdom grand,
You guide us all with gentle hand.

A glance from you, it says it all,
No need for words, no need to call.
In moments shared, we both agree,
The simplest things are the key to be.

So sit and stay, a lesson here,
With every drool, you draw us near.
Your wisdom shines in wag and bark,
A fluffy sage, a loyal spark.

Searching for the Why in Playtime

Why chase that ball, oh furry friend?
Your joy, it seems, has no end.
A stick, a leaf, a squirrel too,
What answers do these games imbue?

In every romp, a mystery hides,
The thrill of joy your heart abides.
You leap and bound with so much cheer,
I watch in awe, my purpose clear.

When toys collide, and squeaks resound,
I grasp the truth in laughter found.
Each wagging tail, each playful bark,
Reveals the why in every park.

So let's embrace this silly quest,
For play brings out the very best.
With every chase, and every grin,
I find my why, and let joy in.

The Universe in a Dog's Sniff

Oh, the secrets in the scents you find,
A world unknown, in your nose combined.
From tree to rock, each sniff a clue,
The universe spills, just for you.

You pause to ponder every whiff,
A cosmic quest, what a gift!
With a wiggle and twist, you dive on in,
Exploring life with a silly grin.

Each paw in dirt, a story tells,
Of canine dreams and playful spells.
In those moments, time stands still,
Just you, the earth, and your nose to thrill.

So let us sniff, both young and old,
In every scent, a tale unfolds.
With tails a-wagging, we'll find our way,
In life's adventure, come what may.

Paws and the Pursuit of Happiness

With every pawprint on the floor,
You trot through joy, forevermore.
A wagging tail lets worries flee,
In your eyes, the world is free.

Chasing dreams, you leap and bound,
My laughter echoes in your sound.
Under the sun, with fur so bright,
You teach me how to bask in light.

Through puddles splashed, and grass so green,
What happiness really means is seen.
With every bark, you share your bliss,
In every nudge, a gentle kiss.

So let's run wild, let spirits fly,
In the pursuit of joy, we'll reach the sky.
With paws beside me, let's embrace this dance,
In the game of life, we take our chance.

Ponderings in the Park

Why chase the ball? It's so far away,
Yet I leap with glee, come what may.
Is it the thrill, or the scent in the air?
Perhaps just a snack that I long to share.

Squirrels dash by, oh what a sight,
Do they reason like us, or just take flight?
I ponder and pause, then I just run,
Life's a big game, and I'm here for fun.

The ducks in the pond quack, just like me,
But do they bark back? Oh, what could that be?
A friendship formed, a grand canine pact,
Or just a good snack moment? That's a fact!

So here in this park, I nibble and roam,
With all my wise thoughts, I call it home.
Every wag of my tail, every bark I lend,
Is just a reminder, life's better with friends.

Sniffing Out the Secrets

I sniff the ground, it's a treasure map,
What secrets lie beneath this grassy flap?
A leftover sandwich or a mysterious bone,
Every whiff tells a story, I'm never alone.

The mailman arrives, I give him a bark,
What's with his bag? It's full, like Noah's Ark!
Does he carry gifts? Perhaps treats, I say,
Or is he just sneaking my chew toys away?

A walk in the park, so much to explore,
My nose is a compass, opening each door.
Every tree is a chat room, every bush a guide,
With you here beside me, I'll never hide.

So let's lift our noses and follow the trail,
Together we're sleuths, we'll never fail.
In this world of scents, we'll always find bliss,
Remember the secrets, with every sniff and kiss.

The Meaning in a Bark

I bark at the moon, what's it trying to say?
Is it a dog's haven, where night meets day?
Or is it just cheese, that floats in the sky?
A slice of the universe, oh me, oh my!

My human looks puzzled, they nod, they grin,
Yet I know the truth that my growl hides within.
With each playful woof, I ask why we're here,
Is it just for the cuddles, or more to cheer?

When I bark at a cat, is it out of love?
Or maybe it's pondering what's up above?
I chase my own tail, round and around,
In circles of thought, nothing profound.

So here I am, scratching my head,
Wondering what's next, after snack and bed.
In each joyful yip, and with every cheer,
I learn my own answers, as sweet life draws near.

Furry Counsel

Oh wise and noble dog, what do you see?
In each wag of your tail, what's your decree?
Should I chase my dreams or chase a new shoe?
You just tilt your head, like it's up to me!

At the window you sit, judging the world,
While I sip my coffee, your paws unfurled.
Is it hard being regal, with such furry grace?
Or do you envy my snacks in this warm place?

You bark at the postman, a fierce little knight,
But the neighbor's big dog is quite a fright.
Yet you wag on, as if it's no fuss,
With every bark whispering, "Trust me, don't rush."

So here we cohabitate, you and I,
With mischief afoot, we give life a try.
In the court of the couch, you reign supreme,
Oh, furry counselor, I'm living the dream!

A Daily Walk Through Questions

Why fret about fate, my friend,
When every squirrel's a chance to bend?
Just sniff the grass and wag your tail,
Forget the worries, let love prevail.

What's with the moon? Is it cheese?
I'll chase it too, if you please!
Just watch my leap, so full of glee,
Together, we hold the key.

Do puddles hide truths we should know?
Jump in and splash! Let feelings flow.
With you by my side, what's unclear,
Becomes a game, joyful and near.

When to sit down, or run and play?
Follow your heart without delay!
Life is short, so I bark in cheer,
Let's explore—your answer's here!

Canine Comfort in Uncertainty

In times of doubt, I hear you sigh,
Why not chase tails 'til the day is nigh?
A tilt of my head, a wagging cheer,
Together we'll conquer, have no fear.

What does it mean to be truly free?
It's all in the treats, don't you see?
The world's our playground, no rules apply,
Just bring that ball and let's fly high!

What if the rain pours, skies turn gray?
Unleash the joy, we'll dance and play!
With muddy paws and a heart so bold,
We embrace every moment, let life unfold.

Do we search for answers, or just some fun?
I'd rather fetch sticks than weigh a ton.
Life's a game where we both can laugh,
Barking together, we'll find our path!

Fetching More Than a Stick

What if the world spins out of control?
Let's fetch excitement, and share a stroll!
Stick or ball, I bring you cheer,
With every toss, the path is clear.

Do bones hold secrets of days gone by?
Watch me dig deep, I'll surely try!
Each find's a treasure, oh so sweet,
With you beside me, life's a treat.

Is happiness hidden in your gaze?
I'll bat my eyes through all the craze.
In every bark, a whisper flows,
Answering questions that nobody knows.

Can the leash tie us? Or set us free?
With you by my side, it's plain to see.
We run or we rest, together we stick,
In this wild world, that's my favorite trick!

The Heartbeat Beneath the Fur

What makes you tick, oh lovely kin?
Is it the treats, or the joy within?
A scratch on the belly, a wagging tail,
In every cuddle, life's details prevail.

Is time just a concept, or friends near?
The best moments are now, my dear.
With every wag, I'm here to say,
Let's relish our time, come what may!

Do you ponder life, as I dream wide?
Join me in chasing the joys inside.
In each goofy leap, and slobbery kiss,
I share with you my canine bliss.

When questions arise, like clouds in the sky,
I'll nuzzle your hand, and we'll soar high.
With a heart that beats beneath the fur,
We'll find answers as long as you stir!

The Simplicity of Fetch

When the ball is thrown, we run in glee,
Chasing joy in every tree.
Why worry about tomorrow's grind?
Just fetch the stick, leave stress behind.

In every leap, there's a lesson true,
Enjoy the moment, it's good for you!
With wags and barks, let laughter flow,
Life's simple games are all we know.

Lessons from the Leash

With a tug, we're off to roam,
Each scent tells tales of the unknown.
Why fret about the road ahead?
Let's chase squirrels instead of dread.

Sometimes we stop, just to explore,
A patch of grass, oh, there's so much more!
Each step a joy, with you beside,
With every walk, adventures collide.

Canine Contemplations

Why do humans wait for the moon?
I prefer a nap, and then a tune.
What's with the fuss about the past?
I roll in grass; joys come fast!

They ponder life with furrowed brow,
While I just bark and take a bow.
A belly rub and treat in hand,
What more do they need to understand?

Tails of Understanding

If I could speak, I'd say with cheer,
'Embrace the mess, forget the fear!'
For every bark and playtime rant,
There's wisdom in a joyful chant.

When storms roll in, just cuddle close,
In silly moments, we find the most.
Life's a park where we run wild,
Ask a pup, and be beguiled!

Questions in the Eyes of a Pup

What is the meaning of a tail that wags?
Could it be snacks are better than rags?
When you leave the room, do you really care?
Or do I just assume you're going to share?

Why do humans talk and not just bark?
Are we all playing hide and seek in the park?
Do you wonder if squirrels have secret plans?
Or are they just plotting to steal my cans?

If I bring you my favorite, does it mean I'm grand?
Or just that I'm hoping you'll give me your hand?
Will you chase the vacuum or just take a nap?
Can we ponder hard before we both take a lap?

So many questions in my little head,
Like why you prefer the couch over a bed?
I'll keep asking, for that's what I do,
Just look in my eyes, and you'll find the clue!

Barking at the Moon: Insights from Canines

When the night sky glows and the stars all twinkle,
Why do I bark? Is it magic, or a sprinkle?
Does the moon ever wonder, or do I just shout?
Can I fetch the stars, or are they too far out?

What's the secret behind that midnight glow?
Is it a giant ball of cheese, or just for show?
When I howl with joy, am I talking to friends?
Or simply expressing where loyalty bends?

If my bark could echo deep through the trees,
Would a squirrel listen? Would he feel at ease?
Maybe the ants would join in my song,
And together we'd hum, it wouldn't feel wrong!

At dawn, I'll rest, with my dreams far and wide,
Chasing the moonbeams, with you by my side.
Tomorrow I'll ask, with that spark in my eye,
For every new mystery, there's more to imply!

The Mysteries Behind a Gentle Nudge

A gentle nudge with my furry nose,
What wisdom lies in this act I chose?
Is it to say, 'Hey, come and play!'
Or perhaps to remind you it's time for the day?

Do you feel my love when I lean so near?
Is my soft touch the reason you cheer?
Have you thought that I'm asking for treats?
Or whispering secrets from our cozy seats?

What if my nudge is an artful quest?
To guide you to dreams, where we've both been blessed?
Or just a reminder, to share your lap?
In the world of a pup, it's all in the zap!

Every nudge holds a story untold,
A mystery wrapped in warmth and bold.
So next time I poke you, just know it's true,
I'm sharing a laugh, or a thought with you!

Dogs and the Meaning of Loyalty

What does it mean to stand by your side?
Is it barking at mailmen, or rolling in pride?
Could loyalty be more than a simple tail wag?
Are there lessons hidden in the way that I brag?

If you lose your way, do I lead the pack?
Or simply show you the way to snack?
When you're feeling down, do I wear a cape?
Or is it just cuddles that help you escape?

Am I your shadow, your guardian too?
Navigating life, all the challenges we brew?
Maybe loyalty's in the way that I cheer,
The playful antics, and being right here.

Together we howl at the moonlit night,
Sharing our dreams, till the morning light.
So here's to the fun and the bonds that stay strong,
Just a pup and his human, where we both belong!

Walking Through the Questions

Why do you stare at the door?
I just want to know what's in store.
The world beyond seems so vast,
But will dinner come first, or will we be last?

Fetch me a stick, oh what a delight!
It's a game, not a duty, right?
With every chase, I ponder my fate,
But your laughter is what truly feels great.

Can I eat that old shoe on the floor?
Is there happiness locked in the door?
Your puzzled face is a sight to behold,
But treats in the pocket are worth more than gold.

Why do humans always sit still?
Is it a game of 'who has the will'?
Just pat my head, and you will see,
I'm always correct when it's just you and me.

The Depths of a Dog's Gaze

In the depths of my eyes, what do you find?
Maybe a secret, or peace of mind?
With a tilt of my head, I ponder a lot,
Is it just me, or have you forgotten the pot?

Can I help you solve your greatest woes?
With a wag of my tail, my wisdom flows.
The answer is simple, no need to stress,
The snack drawer, dear friend, is truly the best.

Every bark is like a riddle of old,
With clues wrapped in fur, and tales to be told.
So after the zoomies and all of the fun,
I'll remind you: together, we've already won!

Look deep in my gaze, and you may just see,
A world of adventures just waiting for me.
What's my next move? Who really can tell?
But sit down with me, and all will be well.

Unfurled Thoughts

Chasing my tail, what a silly quest,
But isn't it fun? I like it best!
Should I share my toys or keep them all?
This philosophical game is a ball!

What if the squirrel really exists?
Do they know about these splendid twists?
With a bark, I ponder the great unknown,
But hey, what's that? The mailman has shown!

Count the clouds, or chase a drift?
The choices abound like a magical gift.
Take a nap or sniff all day?
Every new moment is here to stay.

The world's a puzzle, so bright and grand,
With each wag, I shuffle through the sand.
But in your heart, I so clearly see,
Life's just a romp when you're with me!

Heartfelt Howls

With a howl at the moon, I ask you this,
Does the night sky hold any hidden bliss?
Each bark is a note in our nightly song,
Together we ponder where we belong.

Why do we sit as the stars twinkle bright?
Each wag carries dreams in the soft silver light.
So do I chase thoughts like I chase my tail?
Let's find out on this grand, furry trail.

Fences divide, but my heart is wide,
To leap over boundaries, still by your side.
With every sniff, my spirit takes flight,
In this adventure of pure canine delight.

With each paw on the ground, and bark in the air,
I wonder what answers are truly out there.
So share in my joys, in the moments we feel,
Together we make the ordinary surreal.

Wags of Wisdom in a Chaotic World

When the world feels heavy and gray,
Just watch my pup tumble and play.
With a wag of the tail, he's got it right,
Chasing his shadow, pure delight.

He barks at the moon, a cosmic jest,
For a squirrel's next move, he's always a guest.
In every misstep, a lesson to find,
Just be like my dog, and don't lose your mind.

Stick your head out and feel the breeze,
Let your worries float like fallen leaves.
Life's a game, you can't win them all,
But a belly rub can fix your fall.

So when you feel lost, just give a glance,
My dog will show you how to prance.
With fur and a bark, he'll set you free,
In this chaotic world, just follow me!

The Eyes That See Beyond

Deep pools of wisdom in those big eyes,
They see the world, and it never lies.
With every wag, a story unfolds,
Tales of loyalty and treasures untold.

He spots the postman, it's a grand affair,
A hero arrives, without a care.
Each glance, a question, a secret to share,
In his simple gaze, I find my prayer.

Those big, droopy ears catch every tone,
He knows when I'm happy or feel alone.
Through puppy snuggles and playful yips,
He answers the mysteries, no need for scripts.

So when you ponder all that's unclear,
Just stare in those eyes, without fear.
For in every woof and soulful cry,
My dog knows truths we can't deny.

Embracing the Here and Now

In the grass where the daisies grow,
My dog teaches me to take it slow.
With every sniff and playful leap,
He reminds me of moments, rich and deep.

Chasing butterflies, a dance so sweet,
No worries of tomorrow, no hint of defeat.
A wagging tail is his way of saying,
Live for today, there's no delaying!

Mud on his paws, and a grin so wide,
With every puddle, he laughs and glides.
Forget the past, it's gone like the dew,
In the present, there's always something new.

So let's frolic and roll, without a care,
Take a moment, breathe in the air.
With a bark and a pounce, he shows me how,
To embrace the here, the magic of now!

The Revelations in Every Slobbery Kiss

A greeting so warm, with a slobbery kiss,
Reminds me of moments I wouldn't miss.
With each wet nuzzle, questions dissolve,
In innocence, life's puzzles resolve.

He licks my face like it's a fine wine,
In every drool, a love so divine.
What's better than treats? It's simple, you see,
It's the joy of the now, just you and me.

Amidst all the chaos, and hectic pace,
There's magic in those whiskered grace.
With every wag and playful spin,
He teaches me laughter from deep within.

So savor each slobber, each furry embrace,
For truth lies in love, not a winning race.
In every moment, let joy persist,
It's the little things that truly exist!

The Secret Language of Dogs

When you bark, I hear a song,
A symphony of joy so strong.
With wagging tails and playful spins,
You dance around, and happiness wins.

In every sniff, a tale unfolds,
Of trees and friends and secrets told.
A squirrel's chatter, a cat's sly wink,
This is the world, come on, just think!

Your laugh is like a sunny breeze,
Chasing tails, we do as we please.
Through muddy puddles, off we go,
The universe, in leaps and throws.

Don't fret for what the future brings,
With treats and toys, we'll rule like kings.
Breathe in the grass, take life in strife,
Together, we're joy, this is our life!

Truths Unleashed by Pawprints

Every pawprint shows a path,
Leading to laughter and silly math.
Is the car round or the park a dream?
Let's chase our tails and giggle and scream.

The neighbor's lawn, my canvas wide,
A masterpiece of marks, I take pride.
Rolling in grass, life's simple joys,
Chasing after sticks, with my good toys.

Questions of why? That's for the wise,
I'll fetch the ball and eat the fries!
When life gets tough, we just bark back,
A belly rub will bring joy and slack.

Oh, what's the meaning? I'm not sure,
But a warm sunbeam is the best cure.
Forget the clock, let's play all day,
With sniffs and wags, we'll find our way!

A Dog's Perspective on Existence

I ponder the mysteries of my bowl,
Why is it empty? It plays a role.
Each droplet counts, a precious find,
The quest for snacks, so well-designed.

Philosophy's tough, can't you see?
Should I chase my tail or just let it be?
Running in circles, barking at stars,
The world's my backyard, with space for cars.

What's underneath the couch? What's there?
A world of wonders, just beyond my stare.
Lost shoes and socks, a treasure chest,
The meaning of life? It's all a quest.

In human hearts, I find my place,
A wagging tail, a warm embrace.
The canvas of love is painted bright,
With every woof, I chase my light!

Tails of Enlightenment

Under the sun, we chase our bliss,
Rolling in grass, can't resist this kiss.
The world is vast, but I know where to roam,
In a pile of leaves, I've found my home.

Count the squirrels, laugh at the glare,
The mysteries of life float in the air.
Will the mailman bring treats? I must know,
Or is he a villain? A lively show!

Why analyze when we can play?
Chasing shadows, that's how we sway.
When life gets ruff, find a friend indeed,
Together we'll triumph, fulfill every need.

So let's not fret over the big and grand,
Life's little moments are simply planned.
With every wag, I see the truth,
Together we laugh, with endless youth!

Tails that Tell Tales

When I ponder the universe deep,
My pup just wants to play, not to weep.
With a wag and a bark, he's breaking the mold,
His wisdom's in fetch, if you dare to be bold.

Chasing shadows, he shows me the way,
To enjoy every moment, not just the grey.
A ball that rolls free, just like our dreams,
In the puppy playground, nothing's as it seems.

With a head tilt and bounce, he asks, 'What's your aim?'
I'll live like a dog, with no need for fame.
His joy is infectious; it leaves me in stitches,
In a world of confusion, my dog has no glitches.

His philosophy's simple, and oh, so profound,
Just sniff out the good, and let love abound.
While I ponder my purpose, he chases a cat,
My answers are clearer, thanks to this brat.

Reflections on a Leash

On our walks, oh the sights we behold,
My dog sniffs the ground with stories untold.
'Why the grass turns green after a rain?'
He blinks with a grin, 'Just leap and refrain!'

With his head held high and tail in a spin,
He teaches me patience; it's the joy within.
I often wonder, 'What's next on the road?'
He answers with barks, 'Just lighten the load!'

Through puddles and mud, we joyfully splash,
His laughter is loud, not a moment to rash.
'What's the meaning of life?' I ask in a tone,
He rolls in the grass, 'Let go of that phone!'

As squirrels dart by, sparking great chase,
He reminds me to live with no worry or haste.
Together we ponder, explore, and we play,
He's the sage of my heart, in his own puppy way.

Barking Back at Existence

With a bark and a wiggle, my pup takes a stance,
'What's the secret to joy?' He barks with a prance.
Is it bones or the sunshine, or running so free?
'It's all of those things, just wait and you'll see!'

In the park, he plays with ducks and some kids,
'What's the point?' I wonder, then he flips and he skids.
His answer is simple, with a roll in the dirt,
'Enjoy all the chaos, dive right into the hurt.'

While I sit and I ponder beneath a tall tree,
He's off chasing tails, so carefree and free!
'Why do we worry? What's wrong with a nap?'
He sighs with content, folds into a lap.

In each woof and wag is a lesson so grand,
To find joy in the little things, paw in hand.
As I question it all, he just gives me a grin,
In the game of existence, we both always win.

The Playful Philosophy of Pups

What's the meaning of treats? My dog has it down,
'It's to wag your tail and share joy all around!'
With a jingle of collars, he leads the parade,
His motto is simple, 'Let's joyfully wade!'

Chasing after the mailman, he stops for a sniff,
'What's wrong with a challenge? Just give it a lift!'
With every new friend, his heart opens wide,
'Just meet them with kindness; let love be your guide.'

Scoffing at worries, he jumps in the leaves,
'Why get so serious? Just roll up your sleeves!'
For every big question, he gives me a nudge,
Let laughter and sunshine be the ultimate grudge.

So I follow his lead, with each playful bark,
'In the game of life, just hit your own mark!'
With a heart full of joy, he teaches me well,
That the secrets to happiness, only pups can tell.

The Search for Meaning in Every Wag

In every wag, there's joy to find,
A mystery wrapped in fur, so kind.
Questions float like treats in the air,
Each tail's swing is a cosmic flare.

Dreams of biscuits as stars align,
Is the moon made of cheese, divine?
Chasing shadows, he asks with a glance,
Can I catch the sun if I only dance?

With every bark, there's a truth to tell,
Are humans silly? Oh, can't you tell!
He sniffs the breeze; with wisdom, he knows,
The secret to happiness, let's strike a pose!

So let's ponder while we play fetch,
Does love truly come from a warm soft stretch?
In every wag, and every glance,
The answers await in a playful prance.

From Nose to Tail: A Dog's Inquiry

What lies beyond the garden gate?
Is the neighbor's yard the next great fate?
With a nose to sniff out every clue,
He wonders if they have treats too!

A squirrel darts by, causing a stir,
Can it teach me something? He'll confer.
A wag of his tail shakes the question out,
Is it true a home can be one of doubt?

When a belly rub brings the world to calm,
Is happiness found in a simple psalm?
He nuzzles close to share the thought,
Is love the only lesson that he's sought?

Together we'll ponder beneath the moon's light,
Is there more to chase than in dreams at night?
With every bark, a new lesson prevails,
From nose to tail, he unfurls his tales.

Squirrels and the Secrets of the Universe

The squirrel dashes; what's the rush?
Does it know secrets that make him blush?
A leap through branches, a fluffy tail wave,
Is it wisdom or just the thrill that it craves?

In the chase, he finds pure delight,
Does the universe laugh, or is it polite?
With every bark, mysteries unfurl,
Maybe squirrels hold truths that swirl.

A nose to the ground, he digs for signs,
Are we all just part of grand designs?
As the world spins on, the dog just knows,
Life is about enjoying the throes.

So let's chase squirrels and dance in the grass,
Isn't each moment a reason to pass?
With questions in tow, let's leap and play,
Each secret found makes a brighter day.

Of Bones, Belly Rubs, and Beliefs

A bone in the yard, my sacred treasure,
Is there a better form of pleasure?
With belly rubs, I ponder the great,
Are they a sign of a loving fate?

Do humans wonder about joy and grace?
Or do they lose sight in life's cold race?
A gentle paw prompts thoughts that amaze,
Are we all just here for good belly days?

Under the sun, I spread out wide,
Is happiness simply a warm guide?
With mischief and love, I lead the way,
My doggy wisdom brightens the gray.

So throw me a ball, let's run with glee,
Are we meant to be wild and free?
In this funny world, with its wiggles and barks,
I find life's meaning in joyous sparks.

Lessons from a Leashed Companion

Why chase after things out of reach,
When a squirrel is the ultimate treat?
The couch is best for a cozy nap,
Forget world problems — take a break, and flap.

When they ask you to sit and stay,
Just wag your tail, and they'll be okay.
Bark for joy, don't hold it in,
Every little win is a chance to grin.

Chasing tails is quite the sport,
Dancing round like you're on court.
The leash may tug, but you're so free,
In every moment, just be you, you see?

With treats in hand and balls to play,
Remember, it's all about the fun today.
Sniff the world, let the humor spread,
Wrap yourself in joy like a dog in bed.

The Fetching Truth

Throw the stick, throw it far,
Chase your dreams, be a shooting star!
But when it's lost, don't you pout,
Just dig it up; that's what it's about.

A bone in your mouth is bliss complete,
Why chew on worries or retreat?
When asked the meaning of woof or bark,
Just cuddle close; you leave your mark.

A puddle jump can cure a frown,
Why look for gold when mud's a crown?
The truth is simple, clear as day,
Happiness is just a wag away!

When all feels heavy, and life's unjust,
Roll on the grass, in laughter, we trust.
Play with joy, chase what's bright,
And let the world become your light.

Silent Barking of the Soul

In the park, the sun shines bright,
Chasing dreams brings such delight.
But curled up on a pile of fleece,
You'll find a kind of peaceful peace.

They ponder what it means to play,
I just wag my tail and sway.
Silence speaks more than any bark,
Grab the moment, make your mark.

When they seek wisdom in the night,
I offer cuddles; that feels right.
Let love and slobber guide the way,
In quiet moments, feel okay.

When you're lost, and the way seems long,
Hear my heartbeat; it's where you belong.
Through every pause and playful leap,
The unspoken bond runs deep.

Wisdom Wrapped in a Wag

In every wag, a lesson hides,
Just roll in the grass, let joy be your guide.
Don't fret the small stuff, enjoy the show,
Sniff the flowers, let happiness grow.

A drop of drool can spark a laugh,
There's wisdom found in every half.
When food's served, make no mistake,
Treats are life's sweetest break.

Why worry over what may come?
Embrace the food, the warmth, the fun!
In every moment found so grand,
You'll find the truth was close at hand.

And if it rains, don't hide away,
Grab your raincoat, and dance today!
Let the world see all your sparks,
For wisdom truly lives in barks.

The Simple Joys Explored

Why chase the ball when I can snooze,
The world can wait, I've got no blues.
Let's frolic in grass, just us two,
Joy is simple, in all that we do.

A squirrel runs by, I get all hyped,
But there's a biscuit? Oh, how I'm swiped!
Treats and pats, that's my grand scheme,
Forget the world, I'm living the dream.

The dawn breaks bright, tail wags with glee,
What's waiting ahead? Just you and me.
With every bark, a new thought appears,
Life's little wonders, no room for fears.

So toss that stick, watch me prance,
In each wag, there's a carefree dance.
With sloppy kisses, I say it's true,
The simple joys are best with you.

Heartfelt Licks and Epiphanies

In my dreams, I chase the stars,
But real joy shines in our backyard spars.
With a slobbery kiss, I'll answer your call,
Deep thoughts dissolve—let's have a ball!

When you're feeling low, I'll rest by your side,
My furry comfort, your emotional guide.
I don't need words to convey it well,
A wag of my tail is enough to spell!

Now, do you wonder what life's all about?
Just look at your dog, that's what it's about!
A scratch on the ear makes the world feel right,
In each heartfelt lick, our worries take flight.

So here's an epiphany, quick and clear,
Life's not that complex, I'll lend you my ear.
With love and a snack, we'll conquer the strife,
Just you and me—oh what fun is life!

Chew Toys and Philosophical Dilemmas

What is life without a chew toy?
To gnaw and to munch brings so much joy.
Philosophy's great, but let's not be stuffy,
I'll choose my plush bear over thoughts that are gruffy.

Should we play fetch or bask in the sun?
A complex question, but let's just have fun.
Throw me the ball, I'll chase it with pride,
In games of fetch, my wisdom does hide.

Barking or howling, which is the way?
An age-old question I ponder each day.
But watching you laugh is the answer I need,
With wagging my tail, I've already succeeded.

So chew on this thought, my dear, while you muse,
Life's not a puzzle, just pick and choose.
With a wag and a bite, we'll navigate fate,
You bring the questions, I'll bring the fate.

Embracing the Present Moment

What's to worry? My bowl's full tonight,
Let's live in the now, it feels just right.
Every wag of my tail tells a tale of delight,
In this fleeting moment, the world shines bright.

I chase after shadows and bounce with pure glee,
Time is just a concept, come run wild with me.
The mailman can wait; let's smell the fresh air,
In each little moment, true joy is laid bare.

When the sun shines down, I nap in its glow,
Doesn't matter where, it's just how I flow.
With a belly scratch here, all worries subside,
And each loving glance makes my heart swell with pride.

So let's drop our stress and just soak it all in,
I promise a nuzzle will surely begin.
In the present we thrive, come frolic and play,
With my furry wisdom, we'll seize the day!

In Search of the Unexamined Bark

When you ponder the stars in the night,
Your dog thinks of bones and a good, long bite.
He barks at the moon with a curious howl,
While you debate if it's cheese or a fowl.

The universe swirls in his beady eyes,
To him, it's just squirrels and yummy french fries.
Each wag of his tail, a riddle or clue,
To find the meaning in belly rubs, too.

He doesn't care how the world came to be,
Just fetch me that stick, oh can't you see?
With a wag and a bark, he'll solve all your woes,
In a life filled with treats, where nothing else grows.

So as you ask questions and scratch your head,
Your pup's looking for snacks, not deep thoughts instead.
In the big cosmic plan, he knows you'll agree,
It's all just about love — and maybe a tree.

Canines and Cosmic Queries

Why chase after quesadillas of fate?
My dog looks for crumbs—doesn't care what's at stake.
With each little bark, he ponders the sky,
Is that a big dog or just clouds passing by?

A galaxy full of chew toys, you bet,
His questions are simple, no need to fret.
"Why do humans sigh? What's with all the fuss?"
He just wants to know—"Will you play fetch with us?"

Don't ask him of planets or who makes the rules,
He'll stumble on grass, discovering new schools.
For as long as he's fed and gets some delight,
The mysteries of life don't keep him up tight.

So let's toss that ball, let the cosmos remain,
With slobbery kisses, we'll dance in the rain.
In the realm of the dog, where we feel so free,
The answers are simple, just you and me!

Furry Philosophers Within

In the corners of thought, my pooch lies awake,
Dreaming of treats, and the odd piece of cake.
He ponders the wisdom of sticks that he finds,
And shuffles through ideas with big furry minds.

"What's the purpose of barking? Why chase that darn cat?"
These questions tumble forth with an eager spat.
He contemplates naps like they're top of the list,
As you tick through dilemmas, he barely exists.

He has a keen sense of where all the fun's at,
Be it rolling in grass or a cozy old mat.
With his nose in the wind and his tail in the air,
He teaches us joy brings the biggest of care.

So let's raise a paw to our canine sages,
Who slice through life's troubles in muzzles and gages.
For each woof is a lesson, a playful parade,
In a world full of questions, love's their charade.

Whispers of the Wagging Tail

When pondering pathways, paths to behold,
My dog wags his tail like it's wisdom untold.
His whispers of joy echo loud in my heart,
With every soft woof, a new journey to start.

"Where does that squirrel go when it runs up a tree?"
He tilts his head sideways, so innocent, free.
To him, it's more grand than alephs and beetles,
It's a game of sweet chases, with fuzzy bristled feebles.

He nudges my hand when I ponder too deep,
As if to remind me, there's fun to keep.
With a playful bark, he'll teach you and I,
That the joy of a chew is worth any sigh.

So, let's chase our tail like the wind in our hair,
With laughter and joy, we'll float through the air.
In the grand scheme of things, he's wise as can be,
A tail-wagging guru, just you and me.

In the Company of Canines

When you chase your tail, my friend,
Are you lost or just in the bend?
I bark, I bark, I must insist,
It's all about the joy, not the list.

Fetch the stick, that's the game we play,
Are you winning, or just in dismay?
I'll wag my tail, you'll see it's true,
Happiness is found in the chase we do.

Squirrel tales twist like dreams at night,
Do you feel the thrill, is it pure delight?
With each sniff, a new world's expense,
We ponder life without pretense.

So when you ask about the grand design,
I'll tilt my head, the answer's divine,
Just roll in grass, let worries scurry,
In the chaos, we'll find all the furry.

Wisdom in the Whiskers

With whiskers twitching, I've seen it all,
The ups and downs, the rise and fall.
A nap is the answer to stress and fear,
Dream big, bark loud, spread laughter, my dear.

From biscuits to bones, every piece of chow,
You wonder what's best? Just ask me how!
The secret to joy is simple, you see,
It's not in the bone, but the time spent with me.

Chase the mailman, that's my plan of might,
What's the meaning of life? It's in the bite!
Let's roll in mud, forget all the fuss,
Your worries are silly, let's ride this bus!

So while you ponder the great unknown,
Just scratch my belly, you'll feel at home.
In every wag, wisdom does flow,
The best part of life? Just let it grow!

The Woof of Wisdom

Oh, the bark of the wise is soft but clear,
In every woof echoes love, my dear.
I know you fret 'bout the things you face,
Just toss the ball, let's pick up the pace.

When life gets ruff and shadows creep,
Find solace in the moments we keep.
The world's a buffet, let's take a bite,
With you by my side, everything's bright.

Do you seek answers in the moon's glow?
Like chasing your tail, it's a funny show!
For every question, a wag and a prance,
Life's a dance, so let's take a chance!

So when you ponder the mysteries vast,
Join me in play, make those moments last.
With a sniff and a bark, truths we shall find,
Forever together, our hearts intertwined.

Paws for Reflection

In the glimmer of sun, I take my stand,
What do you want from this vast, wild land?
I wag my tail; it's all quite absurd,
Let's chase butterflies and skip the word.

Every roll in grass is a grand delight,
Asking for answers? Just hold me tight.
A lick on the cheek, and you'll surely see,
Joy isn't found, it's in you and me.

The big questions tear like silly old socks,
But I'll fetch you truth from my treasure box.
Could it be laughter that fills up the void?
In every paw print, your heart's overjoyed.

So glance at me now, as we sit on this log,
The world's not so big when you've got your dog.
Just live in the moment, let worries go free,
In the warmth of this bond, we're happy, you see!

Pawsitive Insights

When you're lost in a thought, just look down,
A wagging tail holds wisdom without a frown.
Chase the sunshine and don't hold a grudge,
Sometimes a squirrel makes it worth the sludge.

Life's a game, fetch is the goal,
Dig deep for joy, make that your role.
Naps are vital, so take them with style,
Woof at the world, it'll make you smile.

Reflections in the Canine Eye

In the gaze of a pup, the answers lie,
What's more profound than a slobbery sigh?
Food is love, that much is true,
Why worry so much? Just chew and pursue.

Sniff the grass, it tells a tale,
Each new smell is an epic trail.
Roll in joy, let the world spin,
Happiness is a dog's best kin.

Solving Mysteries with a Snout

What's behind that door? Just a friend or foe,
A nose knows the secrets, it's never slow.
Digging for clues in the soft, cool earth,
Every day's an adventure, filled with mirth.

Paws print paths where few have tread,
Sniffing out mysteries, enough said.
The mailman's arrival? A thrilling show,
Who needs a puzzle when there's so much to know?

Bones of Contemplation

Bury your worries, let them go slow,
Life's more fun with a bone to throw.
Gnawing on thoughts while lazing in sun,
Every moment is better when shared with fun.

The big questions fade with a wagging tail,
How to be happy? Just follow the trail.
Jump for joy, chase your dreams in a run,
With a bark and a leap, you've already begun.

www.ingramcontent.com/pod-product-compliance
Lightning Source LLC
Chambersburg PA
CBHW051649160426
43209CB00004B/851